THE BOOK OF MIRACLE-1

FIDDAH NAVASUDEEN

To the people who supported and loved me, To everyone who was an inspiration to me, and the ones who hated and hurt me..because they did push me forward to achieve...

My Best friends forever, Ayyu, ma, and pappa!

To the people who su[illegible] and to everyone who [illegible]

an [illegible] the ones who lived and learnt [illegible]

[illegible] to achieve...

[illegible]

Contents

Foreword *vii*

Preface *ix*

Acknowledgements *xi*

Prologue *xiii*

1. Poems 1

2. Quotes 23

3. Essays 29

4. Speech 34

Thank You So Much! 37

Foreword

"I don't think I will ever succeed!"

"If you really work hard and try your best,even if you lose it is considered as victory..work how much ever you can and pray to god,have faith in him,you will win!"

Preface

This Book is full of poems and quotes for peace ,motivation and yeah fun!

Essays and my tedx school level won(speech)

All these are complete original works of the writer(Fiddah Navasudeen) and are copyrighted too!

For sending suggestions / recommendations or contacting the writer:Poet.Writer.fiddah@gmail.com

My instagram account : fiddah_navasudeen

DM anything to me..maybe even how good/bad the book is!

Acknowledgements

Alhamdulillah,Finally achieving something I have dreamed for years..thank God!

My parents have been really supportive doing everything I wish and guiding me throughout this journey,

My brother Ayyu-of course the naughty one has been of some help

My grandparents -Motivating me so much and supporting me when we have fights!

My Maternal grandmother, who is exactly like me with all kinds of wishes in life..

My aunt in Dubai gave ideas and a looong lecture till midnight that made me cry! Anyways learnt something from that though!

My cousins who kept supporting me -Simply even if i was wrong! Of course my favorite cousin I spent so much time with was the sisters…I Don't think I can mention all the cousins' names though,they might be angry at me!

My aunts and uncles for helping me out with things since I was born-my fathers brother(Uncle) for the unforgettable motivation he gave! Well his name-Mubaarak

My teachers who supported me-mrs.Sofiya was just amazing throughout,pushed me to do what I wanted to do!

I loved making new friends but at the same time loved to sit alone at school!

Thanks a lot to the people at school who kept making me happy,who hurt me a lot because that only motivated me,the ones who thought they were the queens!

Yeah,all kinds of people at school…

My friends and a few people who are close to my heart! They know who they are!!

I am so particular when it comes to choosing the best friends! Of course the others are great!

Weird kind of friends-one to only share secrets,one for only laughing…

Thanks to Enas hybrid school in Ghana,it was where I learnt english!

To all the people i have ever met -learnt something or the other from them..

A big Fat Thank you in the end to all of you!

Prologue

Life is just amazing when you realize how blessed you are and what god has given you.

At times we complain a lot for things like I don't have that,I don't want these and so on,

We just forget the value of what we have and just wish for things,simply even if we don't need them or if we don't even have any use,to us what matters is we need to get whatever we wish!

'We' in the sense generally talking about humans,including me but I just realized how important it is to respect the value of the things we have in our hands,rather than just wishing for things,money is earned by working hard by our parents and we just have to use it wisely,we all make mistakes and it's totally fine but to understand it and to change ourselves is really important, I am just a teen who wishes to share things I have learnt. I have heard people compare themselves to others and say "I am really nothing compared to her" and stuff like that. We have to understand each one of us is really really unique and talented in our own way,like I might write,you might play sports, your mom might cook well and so on..each one of us is unique, that is there is no one like an exact copy of us! To compare ourselves with others and feel lowered is stupid and to compare ourselves with others and feel higher is also bad,like too much boastful of what you have or even headweight, and respecting other's ideas or appreciating other's achievements and accepting the truths about their abilities is really essential and never

ever get jealous, I have never felt jealous and I am always happy for others and that's also a reason to be happy in life! You cannot just say "look at her poem that's terrible" when you really liked it. Don't have hate for anyone just love and if you don't love it's fine but don't curse them or wish for something bad to happen to them.There might be a lot of annoying people around us but we'll have to ignore them and do what we wish , live a really amazing life cause you have everything you need, that is feel blessed and always try to be happy. There is always someone above us,watching us and blessing us.Have faith in god and pray to god,for he's the one who gave us everything we love! Always remember the thing , I am supposed to feel joyful and live my life rather than complaining or comparing, feel blessed.

If you follow these important steps in life you'll notice the difference,the change..

First is never compare yourself with others,second is that never get jealous of others, third is always be glad that you have whatever you have, fourth is just follow these and feel blessed and unique,find the real you and your capabilities to do things.I found out that I can write poems and read a lot, and I am utilizing time to develop my abilities and feel blessed and pray to god for thanking for whatever I have and just live well,for you live only once.

The way The world is!

People might be good, might be bad as well…I just wish to share a few things that I felt and learnt in school. I do have friends,supportive parents, a good family and all that! At times I feel lonely and hurt,sometimes too much joy! We all go through all these times. In my life a few instances taught me a lot..like for example there was a time when I really got angry when one of my classmate and her best friend asked me why I have done my hair like that for the comparing assembly, I was surprised, My wish to be what I want and I was all happy about assembly and stuff when they just come to me and in a really rude way they say these words...I was little,like them,the intentions matter to me..if they said that because they cared then it's fine but the way they said was hurting and I just got that angry and said that it was all my wish, I mean this is silly and stupid,at school everyone fights and this is just okay! I forgave them,we all were little kids.That day I learnt however we are they will say such things because they have different opinions and we must not care and it's not our job! Then came instances like in high school where people said I looked like a ghost and I was immature and I ignored and took it lightly and as a part of fun! They say that it was for our sake they said that or so! What bothers me is that it's our wish to be the way that we wish, our life to play with,to spoil and have fun or do anything that can be stupid as well! People pass comments,let it be anywhere...that's annoying and hurtful but they are worth nothing if all they do is to tell mean things to us with bad intentions and when they do nothing to develop them. So, these topics were the most important lessons I learnt and I wished to share them with you all. At the end of the day,I just feel great! Cause you have just read something that can change your life! Remember these words (I DON'T CARE,I DO WHAT I WISH and I IGNORE THE COMMENTS THAT I GET)

1. Poems

Acrostic poems

DOCTORS

D- Determined to save us,

O- Optimistic and each one of them is genuine,

C- Courageous and bold,

T- Trust them,they shine like gold!

O-Oh,the way they care for us!

R- Roses and lilies bloom,

S- Super heroes they are!

DOCTORS

D-Day or night

O-On their sight,

C-Could you ever see,

T- Tiny drop of glee?

O-On their face we see patience,]

R- Red drops of blood are saved!

S- Saving is their life and wishes!

DOCTORS

D-Day or night

O-Optimistic work they do,

C-Caring and daring to us!

T-Together let's show our love

O-Original and pure love

R-Remember their kind hearts!
S-Sympathy is what we must show!
NURSE
N-Neither sleep nor rest
U-Understand their feelings
R-Respect their dedications,
S-Sympathize their love,
E-Energetic angels they are!
VIRUS
V-Vulnerable situation is what we are facing,
I-Isolation is what we are experiencing,
R-Reluctant and restless to wear a mask,
U-Unsure about the future,
S-Social distancing kept us distant!
PAIN
P- Pouring tears and sadness
A- Angry and torn
I - Hurts deep inside
N- No smiles shown, for that's called pain
SORRY
S- Sweet little heart,
O- Optimistic to apologize,
R- Real love is shown
R- Ready to care
Y- Yet No reply for it?
SORROW
S-Sensible little girl

O-Opens her heart to people
R-Ready to live but,
R-Really torn apart,
O-On her face teras roll,
W-Weeping poor little thing
ENERGY
E-Every time I cry,
N-Nothing changes!
E-Everytime I laugh,
R-Reverse happens,
G-God gave great life,
Y-You all must enjoy it!
HURT
H-He or she must,
U-Understand that,
R-Revenge only hurts!
T-Talk,love,solve!

FUN
F-Fire works,it is
U-Under the roof,on a terrace
N-Near some nature!
KILL
K-Knives or guns
I-I don't use,
L-Love,I use
L-Love,I can!

FORGIVE
F-Fiddah never harms,
O-Or hurts or kills!
R-Revenge tears her down,
G-Gifts is all she gives
I-In her heart there is no evil,
V-Victory comes on her way,
E-Enemies she doesn't have,she is one for the world!
YOU DEVIL
Y-Your heart's full of stones and air,
O-Oh Lord,Save me!
U-Under the roof,I'm safe
D-Ditching you is great
E-Enemy,accept that title,
V-Very angry,Can hurt you!
I-I don't do hurting,not me,not like you
L-Love…you donno it's something in soul!
PEOPLE
P-Purple coloured lips or glittery eyes,
E-Everything's just a thing for the world to criticize!
O-Optimistic heart and soul,they don't care!
P-Prepare to face the hate,
L-Live happily they will always hurt you,
E- EVery day they hurt and hate, That's the world!
1 Stanza poem for cats and puppies!
Cats!
Fluffy and white like snow,

Would look fine with a bow!
We hear their meow,
For fried fish and fries..
Puppies!
Cute and furry,
So little and energetic!
To play with,
We are in a hurry!
It makes us fit,
As we keep running behind it,
We always feel dynamic!

Poem 1 :The Almighty
The Almighty is the supreme power,
Watching us every hour!
He is the one who created us,
From tiny germs and worms,
To the beautiful butterflies and flowers,
The planet earth was made by him,
Bot only earth,
But birth and death are decided by him!
Poem 2: Aurora of seasons
During the aurora of Spring,
What a plethora of flowers it brings.
We can see the beautiful scene,
Which shows us a part of paradise,

Butterflies and flowers all around,
Cheerful daffodils singing sound.
We feel like eating lots of fruits,
As it's our gift given by Nature.

During the aurora of Summer,
What a plethora of sunshine it brings.
I feel idyllic and I want to be an ice,
Which makes me feel nice.
As the last bell of school rings,
We feel we have got wings of joy.
Our stomach will be filled with cool drinks,
As we finish them in a blink!

During the aurora of Autumn,
What a plethora of wind blows.
We can see the amusing scene of fall,
When each leaf dances and falls down.
Cranberries and pomegranates,
Juicy and yummy to eat,
We give gifts for thanksgiving Day,
We start enjoying our play.
We are still filled with joy,
Most excited as halloween arrives,
We scare others and have fun!

During the aurora of winter,

We can smell the petrichor
Snow and rain all over,
We feel like a poor beggar ,
Who waits for a plethora of sunshine
Sweaters and scarfs all over us,
Which is really not a fuss.
Hot and tasty coffee ,
Along with a hot and fresh toffee!
Poem 3: By the sea shore
We feel the sunshine,
The wind blowing so fine,
The smooth and free sand,
We run in that same smooth land,
That's really relaxing , let's understand.
Waters moving up and down,
We tend to frown,
As if we were wearing a crown,
The smooth sand in the shade of brown,
But too much far you will drown!
Think, do we get this beauty in town?
We stand by the sea shore,
And enjoy to the core,
Never seen it's beauty before,
We feel we need more,
What's all these beauty for?
It's not for us to ignore,
But to enjoy it's beauty to the core!

By the sea shore,
Never seen before,
We look for big sea shells,
As it's unique and well,
The sea gives us farewell,
We feel doing sea dwell,
By the sea shore
Poem 4: Let's do away with racism
Let's do away with racism,
As it's never our chum,
It shatters us down,
We wouldn't be able to frown.
It makes us fight,
Never gonna be right,
Put away these things off your minds,
Some of the world reminds,
Not to prevail you racism.
I am one of 'em who reminds.
Each and every minds,
Dont ever thing you define,
something so nice and fine,
All you do is hurt,
And this attitude is dirt.
Racism, why are you still alive?
We never want you to thrive,
I would always strive,
To kill you someday,

I won't delay,
To go on my way,
I would convey to each mind
Goodbye racism, go away forever,
You crushed our peace,
And shattered us into pieces,To destroy you I strive
You won't be alive
Goodbye racism.......

Poem 5: My Grandpas
My paternal Grandpa might be old,
But he is too bold!
He hates to scold,
So brave and says to shine like gold,
Oh the life lessons he told,
Made me bold,
And my tears I could hold!
My maternal grandpa is religious,
As well as ambitious,
Never believes in superstitious,
Trained his children to be ambitious,
When I heard That he sings well,I became suspicious,
Hell lot of books he has read,it's prodigious...
Oh how he made his whole generation religious!
My Paternal grandpa motivates a lot,
Believes me, and the things he bought,
Just for me- They are really a lot,

He has also bought me a flower pot,
And so many life lessons he taught,
He says, " there's nothing you cannot!"
Do,just try,believe that there's nothing you cannot.
My maternal grandpa reads,
One classic then again proceeds,
He tells to do good deeds,
My paternal grandpa loves to hear,
Anything I sing, I give speeches, That's clear,
He says I am talented, chill and cheer,
He himself wrote poems and spoke in stages, cheer!
Poem : 6 Never forget the 5th of september
Thy mind ponders the role of teachers,
Every single soul,including the backbenchers
Their hard work is splendid,When you ignore it shatters!
Oh dear! Such a day is a blessing,
Never forget the 5th of september,
Remember that day,the number
For these angels make us shine
All our hearts including mine,
Must show our love and respect,
To them gifts is what they never expect,
Write a poem or make a card!
Rather than a short form text,
That resembles laziness
We aren't sloths, are we?
Lets just spill all our emotions on a wonderful card,

That's what they really love!
Neither a trending text
Nor a few emojis that we use today
Can never be the same as
Those lovely paper cards we make,'
With crayons and our wordings!
My parents always remember this marvellous day
And they are always in touch with their school teachers,
They remind me,
Dear,School days are the best part of your life,
Don't ever waste these precious times
Such a part of your life you'll never get,
Just enjoy these days, and make memories
Scoldings makes us rectify,
Punishments makes us perfect,
Our school days weren't modern like yours,
Not so much of technology we grew up with,
No online classes or smartphones all the time!
But something common even today,
TEACHERS!who made our childhood marvellous!
Who make your childhood marvellous
These words,My parents told, made me think
So, Show respect and love for them
Never forget the 5th of september,
Oh dear, Dazzling stars always do have,
Memorable moments with teachers,
They say nothing is impossible,

Dear just try and make it possible,
And all we can say is ineffable teachers we have got,
I really feel that I have made a memory at school,
Each and every day!
From my first day to school,
Till now, I feel so cool,
That i really want to remain like this,
Playing, learning and making friends.....
These days will just past by,
Teachers make it wonderful memories for us,
An epic adventure with joy,
Fun,blackboards,benches,punishments and what not?
Never forget this day!
Flowers are beautiful and fragrant,
But they just don't stay the same always,
They dry and dry and fall someday!
They are fabulous, of course!
Leaves dry and fall the same way too!
But dear, wonderful memories just stay,
Deep inside our hearts,our thoughts...
It's always with us , forever!
We just wear an emotional smile,
When we flip through the pages of an old album,
With memories of school life and teachers....
Remember our whole supporting and guiding angels!
Even when tears come rolling down,
They comfort us and say dear child you mustn't cry!

As a poet, I will write and write for my beloved teachers,
Never forget this wonderful day!

POEM:7 One of my passions

Bound by young fold mountains,
With mighty rivers flowing through it.
Surrounded by countries and ocean
Oh! Thy mind would be filled with peacefulness.
Those beautiful landscapes,trees and seas!
Each state with unique nature,
Wonderful diversities and culture!
With many talented people,
Vast variety of flora and fauna,
Each one of us aims to make our nation thrive.
Through our talents and passions,
Such a beautiful country we live in!
Let's join hands to make our nation flourish,
It's one of my passions,

I am so keen,
To make my nation serene.
I would make this my routine,
As I always wanted our nation to remain as a queen!
Let's make our nation more green,
From Andhra's neem trees,
To West Bengal's Alstonia,

Are all our gifts of nature.
All we have to do is conservation.
To make my nation thrive and flourish,
Is one of my passions

I would really strive to provide education,
For each and everyone in our nation,
And completely demolish discrimination.
Youth's education is a key for next generation
My emotions and expressions is what I write,
Every girl's discontinuation of education,
Destroys their passion!
One book and a pen can empower our nation,
That's an educational power.
Our talents and skills are tools!
Every women wants our nation to cherish
They chive when their feelings are shattered by people.
To empower women,our talents are the power!
To develop my nation,
Is one of my passions.
This poem isn't mumbo-jumbo,
With all my might and main,
I would make our nation thrive.
I am a teen who's so keen,
To develop our nation who's a queen!

To develop my nation is one of my passions.

Poem:8 Stand for Equality
Let's not be quiet,
But stand for our right,
Let's raise our voice,
And make a choice,
Let's bring equality.
As it's our necessity!
Let's not be quiet,
But stand for our right,
Fight for equality,
And show our capability,
Let's stand together,
Forever and ever!
Let's not be quiet,
But stand for our right,
Don't be worried,
As equality is all we need,
Let's lit our lights,
And stand for our rights!

Let's not be quiet,
But stand for our right,
Let's be like stars that shine,
And everything else would be fine,
Let's stand for peace,

Rather than making war,
But equality is all we need!

Let's not be quiet,
But stand for our right,
Be joyful!
Don't be mournful,
But be cheerful
And stay spiritual!

Let's not be quiet,
But stand for our right,
They must show gentleness,
And politeness,
So we throw our sadness,
And never become spiritless!

Let's not be quiet,
But stand for our right,
Let's not be negligent,
But be vigilant,
We have to variegate,
Let's stand together

Let's not be quiet,
But stand for our right,
Let's find out a way,

For all this,anyway!
Come one let's do it,
It's not greed but a need!

Let's not be quiet,
But stand for our right,
Why do we need to fight?
Let's solve it,anyway!
Let's not be quiet,
Throw away your fright!
Poem: 9 Butterflies of spring
Beautiful butterflies,
Flying all around the garden,
Their beauty reduced my burden,
Shades of colors,
And adorable wings…
Joy is what it brings,
Flies all around the flowers..
Spreading happiness,
So amazing to our eyes,
We can't hear their cries,
As it's always busy,
Making us happy!
Beautiful butterflies,
Flying all around the garden,
But at times it has no freedom,
You know why?

It's wings is what we use,
To make a place colorful!
It flies freely,
But dies unreasonably!
It cannot raise its voice,
As it's freedom is our choice,
It's wings attracts us,
And spread beauty!
They are pretty ,
We all know it!
Collection of these suns fun,
We aren't harming just one,
But in numbers and numbers!
Makes us feel superb,
But why do we disturb?
They are more valuable,
Than a costly gem!

Poem : 10 Flowers
Fantastic Flowers
Fabulous colors
Attractive petals
It's fragrance is realistic,
White colored lilies,
Rose petaled lotuses,
Bright yellow disked daisy,

These flowers are so glossy!
Beds of flowers for all fragrant lovers,
Different shades of colors,
We gift them as they show great honor!
Different colored tulips,
Bright yellow daffodils,
Brown disked sunflowers,
All are fantastic!
Fantastic and Fabulous,
Colors and petals,
Found in beds,
Found in gardens,
Fabulous fragrance....
Poem:11 Juicy fruits
Juicy and yummy,
Sweet as sugar,
Healthy and valuable,
Live a long happy life!
Red strawberries and cherries,
Which are sweet and sour.
Makes you feel cool during summer,
That's Mr.melon..
So tasty, keep eating but no harm
Nature's sweet and yummy gifts,
We should be grateful and thankful...
Pour happiness and dance around!
Mouth watery and delicious,

Different tastes and colors,
Natural and fresh,
Pluck them and enjoy the taste,
Without any haste!

Poem:12 SOIL IS WHAT WE SPOIL!

Soil is what we spoil,
But that's not an issue we feel!
Be dynamic,save our dear friend,
Who is the reason for our life!
Soil is what we spoil,
Life without soil,
No plants, no breath..
EVery breath possible by it!
But why do we spoil?
Soil is what we spoil,
From tiny ants to huge animals,
Every life needs you-soil!
We must feel sorry,
We'll ensure to save you!
Soil is what we spoil,
Save soil and save your own life!
Even a small portion is useful,
BE careful but more smartful!

POEM 13: My sweet Family

My mom is a great cook,
Who taught me how to read a book!
My dad taught me to be bold,
He wants me to shine like gold!'
My little brother taught me to be cool,
Just like the water in the pool!
My sweet little Family!
Poem 14: My little Brother
My little brother is a naughty one,
Without him there won't be any fun!
I spend my time with him every day,
DO you know why?
To begin my beautiful day!
My little brother is a funny boy,
Who keeps playing with a toy…
I love my little brother forever and ever!
Poem 15: The Almighty
The Almighty is the supreme power,
Watching us every hour!
He is the one who created us,
From tiny germs and worms,
To the beautiful butterflies and flowers,
The planet earth was made by him,
Bot only earth,
But birth and death are decided by him!
Poem 16 : My lovely Garden
My garden is beautiful and lovely,

Full of fruits and flowers,
We all play together,
Have lots of fun and run all around!
A place which makes you calm and quiet,
My lovely Garden,
Beautiful and wonderful!

2. Quotes

"If I see a girl,I might think she's talented and beautiful but I never think that I wish I was like her.."

"This world is really becoming a bad place to live,But if a person can keep his/her heart as an amazing place,then there's nothing better"

"To say I have something is more powerful than saying if I had something.."

"I strongly believe that all are talented but is it necessary to show off and boast about these talents?

"My brother is a person who is cool and happy,I learnt so much from him.

" What is life without a brother? To me brother means so much."

I have met many people,one was really interesting because they used me well...I still kept helping them not because i was a fool but there was no reason for me to follow their character"

"To me mothers are heroines and Fathers are heroes."

Work harder and leave the rest to god,he'll decide if we should win or lose,for we have to fail at times.

"She is more than me and I am nothing compared to her or everyone is lower than me and I am the best-These two sentences are the true definitions of foolishness and head full of flies..

"You decide who you are and what you can do,just take the good things others say.."
"Girls Gossip,we hear it often,we can correct it by saying not all girls gossip!"
"Something that I won't be able to buy is boldness from great people like my father.."
"Never think there is no one for you, there will be someone who will understand and support you!"
"If your heart is broken into two pieces, you can put it back by using the bold glue!"
"I feel a paper and a pencil is far more better than laptops and phones"
"Offline is more fun than the online ways"
"Fake friends are dangerous and finding good ones is a solution"
"Money is really important to survive but life isn't completely about money,some things do not require money!"
"We all have to face death someday,life is never permanent so live your life as you wish"
"Money is the guest that brings both tension and joy to our houses!"
"Bath to have a clean body and pray to have a clean heart in life"
"People keep saying I am not good at something,when I know what I can do, why would I ever listen to those?"
"I have met so many people in my life,and I learnt not all are going to be on your side or just be as you wish,people are how

they are and we cannot change them!

"' People tell me I am horrible at speeches,I am not good at that and so on .... but I know who I am and why should I ever listen to those!

"' I have met a person who always comes behind me for help,needs and never ever care for me when I need something, but still I keep helping that person not because I am a fool but thats my character and there is no need for us to follow someone else's characters!"'

"' I always thought about other people's comments about me, What will they think about me if I lose,If I cry, if I and so on.... My mom Told people think so much and we can never ever try to change or stop their thoughts! That changed me, supported me,made me happy and yes...so much change!'

"So many people of this world work for something,win, Some happily accept all true comments, Some look at negative comments and fall down,Some just take good ones deep inside,Some just look through both and take what's needed! Think which category you belong to!"

"People try to be who you are,but remember something: they can only take you as their role model but never be you!"

"Focus on what makes you happy not on what makes others happy"

"Anybody with a hardworking soul and good intentions can achieve"

"Being alone is not something to feel bad about,rather you can explore yourselves and focus on your goals."

"Sometimes I feel like never have good friends,but taking the positives of people is healthier than their negatives"

"People will always judge you no matter what,but it is you who decide if it should take so much of your time and energy!"

"If you have a broken heart,fixing it is clever and letting it break more is stupid"

"When somebody tries to let you down,or hurt you all you'll feel like doing is something as a result of anger but when you stay calm and walk always the results are great!"

"The funniest thing about the people who are jealous of you is they keep burning inside when you keep winning"

"Never try to please a person,once I tried to but then I found out that there isn't any use since the person isn't fit for it,I wasted time in pleasing and proving people,never do that!"

"It can be anyone in front of you but there isn't any need to prove them your worth!"

Sometimes we feel like we aren't enough or we always come up with a lot of insecurities but then someone out there looks at you and says "you have no idea how much you are worth" and then you just realize how much mistake you have made!"

"Everyone's pretty,no one's called ugly, it's just that we are unique in our own way!"

"Sometimes we try to focus on the negativity in our lives rather than the blessings but that can cause only failure in many ways!"

"Trying to change who you are just to prove or please others isn't healthy at all!"

"It's not just a boy who can achieve but also a girl,it's no just a white can achieve but also a black or anyone for that matter,it's not just that a non-hijabi can achieve but a hijabi too, it's not just a particular person who can achieve but ayon with a kind hardworking heart!"

"If I wear something it's completely my wish,there are people out there walking naked,but when people wish to cover themselves it's called so many terms.. trying to act like a big queen or king by deciding what others should wear is rubbish."

"What bothers you if I wear something that I like?"

"It's not fair how some people still act without kindness,discriminate and it shows how less educated they are!"

"People might give weird looks when you wear hijab,just keep your head straight,do what you wish because they are just woods with stones as hearts"

"If you are a muslim you are terrorist,if your a white you are racist,if you are black you are not worth it,if you are a hijabi you have no beauty,if you are a girl you cannot achieve….these statements show how poor the world must be in education."

"If somebody gives you a glare, give them a big wide smile in return,they might now how evil they are"

"I felt that sometime we'll have to wait for good things to happen"

"Praying helps you reach great heights"

"Bible or quran, hindu or muslim we all are of same kind,living in the same world,drinking the same water"

"If a person is evil it has nothing to do with religion,they are bad not their religion,they just don't follow the rules"

"If you feel you are better than everyone you are wrong,push those thoughts away!"

3. Essays

Feel blessed about yourself

Life is just amazing when you realize how blessed you are and what god has given you.
At times we complain a lot for things like I don't have that,I don't want these and so on,
We just forget the value of what we have and just wish for things,simply even if we don't need them or if we don't even have any use,to us what matters is we need to get whatever we wish!
'We' in the sense generally talking about humans,including me but I just realized how important it is to respect the value of the things we have in our hands,rather than just wishing for things,money is earned by working hard by our parents and we just have to use it wisely,we all make mistakes and it's totally fine but to understand it and to change ourselves is really important, I am just a teen who wishes to share things I have learnt. I have heard people compare themselves to others and say "I am really nothing compared to her" and stuff like that. We have to understand each one of us is really really unique and talented in our own way,like I might write,you might play sports, your mom might cook well and so on..each one of us is unique, that is there is

no one like an exact copy of us! To compare ourselves with others and feel lowered is stupid and to compare ourselves with others and feel higher is also bad,like too much boastful of what you have or even headweight, and respecting other's ideas or appreciating other's achievements and accepting the truths about their abilities is really essential and never ever get jealous, I have never felt jealous and I am always happy for others and that's also a reason to be happy in life! You cannot just say "look at her poem that's terrible" when you really liked it. Don't have hate for anyone just love and if you don't love it's fine but don't curse them or wish for something bad to happen to them.There might be a lot of annoying people around us but we'll have to ignore them and do what we wish , live a really amazing life cause you have everything you need, that is feel blessed and always try to be happy. There is always someone above us,watching us and blessing us.Have faith in god and pray to god,for he's the one who gave us everything we love! Always remember the thing , I am supposed to feel joyful and live my life rather than complaining or comparing, feel blessed.

If you follow these important steps in life you'll notice the difference,the change..

First is never compare yourself with others,second is that never get jealous of others, third is always be glad that you have whatever you have, fourth is just follow these and feel blessed and unique,find the real you and your capabilities to do things.I found out that I can write poems and read a lot, and I am utilizing time to develop my abilities and feel blessed and pray to god for thanking for whatever I have and just live well,for you live only once.

The way The world is!

People might be good, might be bad as well…I just wish to share a few things that I felt and learnt in school. I do have friends,supportive parents, a good family and all that! At times I feel lonely and hurt,sometimes too much joy! We all go through all these times. In my life a few instances taught me a lot..like for example there was a time when I really got angry when one of my classmate and her best friend asked me why I have done my hair like that for the comparing assembly, I was surprised, My wish to be what I want and I was all happy about assembly and stuff when they just come to me and in a really rude way they say these words…I was little,like them,the intentions matter to me..if they said that because they cared then it's fine but the way they said was hurting and I just got that angry and said that it was all my wish, I mean this is silly and stupid,at school everyone fights and this is just okay! I forgave them,we all were little kids.That day I learnt however we are they will say such things because they have different opinions and we must not care and it's not our job! Then came instances like in high school where people said I looked like a ghost and I was immature and I ignored and took it lightly and as a part of fun! They say that it was for our sake they said that or so! What bothers me is that it's our wish to be the way that we wish, our life to play with,to spoil and have fun or do anything that can be stupid as well! People pass comments,let it be anywhere…that's annoying and hurtful but they are worth nothing if all they do is to tell mean things to us with bad intentions and when they do nothing to develop them. So, these topics were the most important lessons I learnt and I wished to share them with you all. At the end of the day,I just feel great! Cause you have just read something that can change your life! Remember these words (I DON'T CARE,I DO WHAT I WISH and I IGNORE THE COMMENTS THAT I GET)

No One is Ugly

We all are creations of God

It means we are wonderful, and we must feel happy about ourselves no matter what.The way our features are,the way our race is,the way we are! yes,I mean everything is a gift,we must always think of people who do not have the things that we have in our lives,Finding out our insecurities and judging is what people will always do,we must prepare ourselves to face that and tell ourselves that there is nothing called insecurities…it's just something that we create,we make and just keep telling ourselves that we aren't enough.Let's just say that we are blessed but we do not appreciate it. We call people ugly,we tend to offend them by saying such words…knowingly or by mistake! The word Ugly does not define anyone…I wonder why that word is actually used.Some think they are the beauty queens and others are not worth it and that they are ugly.We all are beautiful in our own ways and there is no need for us to hide ourselves from this world.Be you and that's the beauty,nothing can define us as anything like ugly or so.Sometimes we feel like others or someone is more pretty than us or such negative thoughts about ourselves...that take most of our happiness or even time for that matter, but thats again stuupid thoughts cause we all know our worth.Don't judge others someday it will come back to us,haunt us make us feel bad and regretted! SO never feel bad when someone judges you and never judge anyone!!

4. Speech

My Speech that got me first place at school....with the help of muslim youtube channels and information I was able to come up with my thoughts in such an order!

Prophet Moosa/moses and the red sea
'I am Fiddah, a 13 year old writer who loves learning about events that occurred in the past and I have heard so many wonderful events like that!' Today I am here to share one such event and I am really thankful to be here and share that with you all..
It's all about mummification and the science behind it. As you all know this process is the culture of Egyptians , where they preserve the dead bodies in the belief of afterlife.This whole process is completely scientific that is each step had a reason and a main aim that is to preserve the dead bodies.The process goes like this... applying natron salt and resin to protect from moisture and decaying , wrapped with layers lenin , placed in coffin and sealed in the tomb, So it was religious as well as scientific. Not all bodies were mummified but the important people of the society like kings and so on . There were so many famous mummies and remesses 2 was one such mummy who was related to another such event "Mosses or Moosa crossing the red sea". He was such a powerful mummy during that

time and I will just give a glimpse of the story about Musa so that you all get an idea of how the king died (ramesses ii). It is mentioned in the Quran and Bible about musa crossing the red sea. In islam it is beleived that Prophet Musa was sent by god to spread monotheism - That is to worship one god, and save the Israelites. The pharaoh refuses to obey God's words and behaves harshly with the slaves and doesn't accept monotheism. Musa and the Israelites were chased by the king and soldiers , Musa came and reached in front of the huge and deep red sea, If I was in such a situation I would have definitely not known what to do, He did not know what to do but God instructs Musa to walk through the sea, Following his words they all just walked across the sea and reached the other side as well, the king tries to do the same but drowns... While drowning he understood his mistake for hating god and behaving harshly, but no point in that as God did not forgive such a sinner. This is completely religious belief , so talking about science his body was then mummified as per tradition and in 1851 there was a need to transport this body to France as it was getting spoilt, To me it Sounds funny as today alive people don't get treatment at proper time due to various issues but in that event a dead body gets treatment in France. Doctor Maurice Bucaille was the one who examined the pharaoh's Body. He is a doctor and a person who always relates religion and science.He was surprised to find traces of sea salt as in the process of mummification sea salt wasn't used at all it was natron salt, then how come? After all his research he related the event of musa/moses and so death of the pharaoh is by drowning in the red sea, that's quite clear! In Quran it is mentioned that his body will be preserved till the end of the world (and yes it is preserved even today)to get his punishment and as an example to all the evil people who hates islam or god. That's all religious so talking about science, The whole process of mummification and each and every step , the red sea and pharaoh was all religious and scientific. Even during those days science was applied , it is being applied and will be applied in the future , Isaac Newton has also said that he was just an ordinary man but application brought success to his life. I would like to conclude what I wished to share and I am really thankful to be able to share such a miraculous event and I just hope you all were able to take away something from what I spoke . Thank you so much

Thank You So Much!

Thank you!

This was book 1 ….the next will be published soon!

Hope you learnt at least a few good things or got ideas on writing poems!

DO send your concerns regarding the book via Instagram or the shared details!

A big thanks to spend your time reading this!!!

Printed by Libri Plureos GmbH in Hamburg,
Germany